SHOULD I ?

Bible Answers to Questions of
Personal Separation

Jim Jorgensen

DEDICATION

This book is dedicated to
my dear wife, Marilyn Hixson
Jorgensen. From the time we
met in our early twenties, she
has been a consistent, unwa-
vering example of a separated,
spiritual Christian. She has a
personal walk with God, and

Jim & Marilyn Jorgensen

she daily lives out these convictions concerning separation as
they are ones she has embraced as her own as well. Her love and
dedication to me, our children, the ministry and our Savior are
an example for others to follow. Her steadfast life and testimony
enforce and exemplify every aspect of the principles I have
shared in writing this book.

First Printing: 2016

ISBN: 978-0-9975624-0-8

FUNDAMENTAL BAPTIST PUBLICATIONS
Lexington, Kentucky

Copies may be ordered through our website at
fundamentalbaptistpublications.com

Printed and Bound in the United States of America

TABLE OF CONTENTS

SHOULD I?

PART 3
CONCLUDING THOUGHTS

Praise for the Book
Should I?

I am very glad to recommend this book on Biblical separation written by Dr. Jim Jorgensen, my friend and colleague since 2003. I do not know of a book or subject that is of a greater need today than this book that deals with the subject of Biblical separation. Dr. Jorgensen deals with what the Bible states about the various areas of the Christian life that are to be noticeably different than that those of the unconverted world. We call this "Biblical separation." He teaches from a Biblical and practical standpoint as to why Christians are to abstain from worldly behaviors, appearances, and practices. In this day and age when many have forsaken the important doctrine of separation, the truth of this doctrine is still very important.

The doctrine of separation is important because our personal testimony of behavior, dress and attitude is vital to be an effective witness and soul winner in our day. Our testimony is what people think of us. Our personal testimony is our qualification for witnessing as to what Christ has done and is doing in our life. Our testimony is either strengthened or ruined by our daily behavior as a Christian.

Dr. Jim Jorgensen has been serving in ministry for more than forty years. Most of that time he has been in the executive leadership of Bible college work. In those years he has effectively and kindly taught personal Christian Biblical standards of dress and behavior to the young people of those Bible colleges.

I enthusiastically recommend this book to you and to your friends.

– Dr. Jeffery J. Fugate, Pastor
Clays Mill Road Baptist Church
Founder and President
Commonwealth Baptist College
Lexington, Kentucky

Thank you for your book *Should I?* on the subject of Biblical separation! Wow, I am excited! I am a book lover and a book owner. I have over 4,000 books in my personal library, but this book fills a crying need. This book clearly explains our convictions from the Scriptures. Dr. Jorgensen has been my colleague and dear friend for more than forty years. He lives what he preaches. Every Christian library and every Christian home should have this book. Again, I say, "Wow!"

– Dr. Wendell Evans, President Emeritus
Hyles-Anderson College
Crown Point, Indiana

This book is timely for the day in which we live. It is a must read for any born-again Christian and a tremendous example for anyone who serves in the ministry of our blessed Lord. It is full of truth from a man who can be trusted and who has lived this throughout his ministry. For many years he has taught thousands of college students in the field of Christian education. Thank God for the great example of Dr. Jim Jorgensen and his Biblical stand on separation.

– Dr. Randy Taylor, Evangelist
West Union, West Virginia

This is a book written by a principled man who has lived out his convictions and standards for the space of a long and fruitful ministry. In its pages you will see the logic and Biblical counsel that my dear friend has taught to others throughout his ministry. Few men could speak with the conviction that comes from a life that has spoken more loudly than his written words.

Agree or not, you cannot but be helped as he makes the case for strong Biblical standards. May these words be used of God to pull us all to a higher standard of living based upon the Biblical principles given in these pages. Dr. Jorgensen is a man among men!

– Dr. Mike Mutchler, Pastor
Grand View Baptist Church
Beavercreek, Oregon

I have known Dr. Jorgensen since the late 1970s. Reading through this book, I find it is as consistent as Dr. Jorgensen

SHOULD I?

himself: scholarly, yet an easy read; logical, and filled with Scripture. This book is definitely one upon which the next generation of Christians can base their philosophies of life and ministry.

– Dr. Bruce Goddard, Pastor
Faith Baptist Church
Wildomar, California

I am writing to recommend this needed book by Dr. Jim Jorgensen titled, *Should I? Bible Answers to Questions of Personal Separation.* It is concise, practical, and laced with solid Bible principles that will help sincere Christians determine how to establish Biblical standards in their lives. I especially enjoyed the foundational principles on which he builds his case. I am also very impressed with the sincerity and the consistency of this fine man over the decades that I have known him. This is a must read in the last days of looseness and self-indulgence.

– Dr. Dennis Corle, Editor
Revival Fires!
Claysburg, Pennsylvania

ABOUT THE AUTHOR

James S. Jorgensen was reared in a good, moral Lutheran home in Racine, Wisconsin. After graduating from a large public high school, he attended Princeton University on a full-scholarship. At Princeton, he earned a Bachelor of Arts degree with a major in mathematics. He then attended Tennessee Temple Seminary under the leadership of Dr. Lee Roberson. He taught math and Greek in the college while attending seminary classes. He received the Master of Divinity degree from Temple and was ordained as a Baptist preacher by Highland Park Baptist Church. While he was in seminary, he met and married his wife, the former Marilyn Hixson. He and his wife have three married children and nine grandchildren. After serving a year as an assistant pastor, he resumed college work by moving to Hyles-Anderson College. There he later received a Doctor of Divinity degree.

Dr. Jim Jorgensen has been a Bible College administrator for over 40 years. He is currently executive vice president of Commonwealth Baptist College. He formerly served as vice president of Hyles-Anderson College and Golden State Baptist College. He has taught and counseled many thousands of students. On any given Sunday, over 1,000 men that he has had a part in training stand to preach the Word of God. He has taught Bible standards throughout this time.

SHOULD I?

In addition to his work in academics, he has been and continues to be a bus worker and a soul winner. He and his wife have been bus workers for over 35 years. To this day, they visit together on bus routes in Lexington almost every Saturday they are in town. They also travel, and he preaches in 40 to 50 churches a year. He has preached in 39 states and 3 foreign countries.

PREFACE

Some may wonder, "Why would you write a book on separation? There are so many different ideas; it will not be accepted by everyone." I believe the answer to the question of why I chose to write this book will be explained in the first chapter, where I explain the Biblical purpose of separation. Since separation is such a basic principle in the Word of God and so important to God, then that principle deserves to have people explain its purpose, principles, and applications to others.

I was reared as a Lutheran in a good moral home. I went to a large public high school (700 in my senior class) and was friends with the "class leaders" in the school. I was one of three candidates to be vice president of the student body during my senior year. I was on the wrestling team, knew the athletes, and ate lunch with the quarterback of the football team most days. I was moral and clean, but most, if not all, of the standards that distinguish independent fundamental Baptists were not a part of my upbringing. I have developed these standards on my own by reading the Bible and listening to other Christians explain them. I did not start with these ideas; I found them in the Bible.

However, as I have started studying the matter of separation more in recent years, I have come to realize it is one of the central doctrines of the Bible. It is one of the keys to having God's blessing on my life or yours. The purpose of this book on separation is much greater than explaining why a Christian should not drink alcohol (although I will cover that and many other specific matters). The purpose of the book is to explain the doctrine of separation, the reason for it and the principles that underlay it.

After we do that in the first several chapters, I will deal with specific matters of personal separation. I have been a teacher and administrator in Bible colleges for over 40 years. During this time, many students have asked, "Why don't we do the things that everyone else does?" In the latter portion of this book, I will give you the Biblical and logical answers I have given these students.

Many in Christianity would say the topic of separation and Bible standards is not important and that we should only separate over "doctrine." The implication is that the only issues worth separating over are the essentials of the Christian faith such as the deity of Christ, the virgin birth, the Trinity, and the blood atonement. Certainly, if someone is wrong on these, he is not a Christian. However, the word *doctrine* means "teaching," and the same Bible that teaches the deity of Christ also teaches standards of holiness and separation from worldliness. While someone can be saved and get drunk, that does not mean that we should say nothing about that behavior. You cannot read your Bible, even casually, and not see the importance to God of separation and holiness.

PART 1

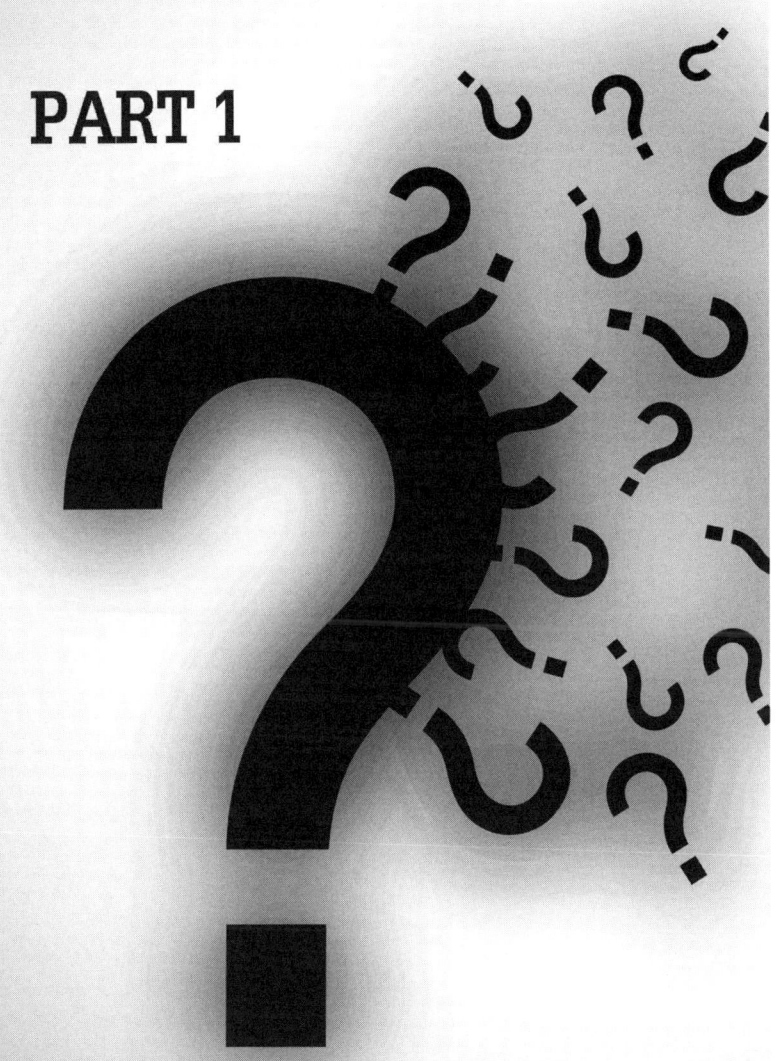

Basic Bible Teaching
Concerning Separation

CHAPTER ONE

THE PURPOSE OF SEPARATION

The purpose of our existence is to glorify God and to fulfill His purpose for our lives. The purpose of separation is to allow us to achieve that goal! **We were created to glorify God, bring praise to Him, and serve Him.**

I Corinthians 10:31 says, *"Whether therefore ye eat, or drink, or whatsoever ye do, do all to the glory of God."*

Colossians 3:17 says, *"And whatsoever ye do in word or deed, do all in the name of the Lord Jesus, giving thanks to God and the Father by him."*

Colossians 3:23 says, *"And whatsoever ye do, do it heartily, as to the Lord, and not unto men."*

Everything I do should be to bring glory to God and for Him. Again, the purpose of my existence is to glorify God and fulfill His purpose for my life.

If I am going to pursue this purpose for my life, then I must separate from anything that would keep me from that goal. That is the reason for Biblical separation. If a farmer wants to raise a good crop, he separates it from insects and weeds. If an athlete wants to win a championship, he separates himself from certain foods and actions that would hinder him. If a pianist wants to improve, he sets aside a time to separate from other activities so he can practice his instrument. We commonly say, "You can't love flowers without hating weeds."

SHOULD I?

According to the Word of God, I am to be "holy as God is holy" (Leviticus 11:44, 45). This admonition is quoted and repeated to New Testament Christians in I Peter 1:14-16. God's standards for holiness in His people have not changed. I was created in the image of God (Genesis 1:26), so I should be holy since God is holy! I Thessalonians 4:3 states, *"For this is the will of God, even your sanctification...."* I Thessalonians 4:7 states, *"For God hath not called us unto uncleanness, but unto holiness."* It is God's will that we be sanctified and holy!

The Bible word *holy* has the same meaning as "sanctified." The essential idea behind both words is *to be separated for a purpose.* In the Old Testament, many objects were called "holy." These would include the oil for anointing, the furniture in the tabernacle, and the furniture for the temple. These physical objects were *sanctified* (or "set apart") for a special purpose. That setting apart made them holy. Here, these words are used of the furniture for the tabernacle. When the objects were sanctified, it clearly did not have to do with taking away sin; the words are applied to physical objects that cannot sin. However, the objects were set apart for that special purpose—and that is the basic meaning of sanctification or of being holy.

So here we are at the very beginning of trying to achieve the purpose for our existence. We realize we must be holy for God is holy, and that means to be set apart for a purpose. **When I was created and again when I was saved, I was set apart for a special purpose that God had for me. I must separate myself from anything that would keep me from fulfilling these goals for my life.**

18

Some seem to think that the standards we have as independent Baptists are arbitrary. "It just depends on how you were brought up," they say. But it does not! The following is probably the most important sentence in this book. **"The list of things from which we should separate is not an arbitrary list, but a list of things that would hinder us in fulfilling the very purpose of our creation, which is to glorify God."**[1] I believe that we should not steal, commit adultery, drink alcohol, take drugs, gamble, smoke, dance, etc., not simply because we are independent Baptists but because these things will hinder us in the purpose of our existence, which is to glorify God!

---

[1]Jack Hyles, *Biblical Separation* (Hammond: Hyles Publications, 1984). Chapter 1 clearly explains this idea.

CHAPTER TWO

THE FOUNDATION OF SEPARATION

As Christians, *all* **that we do in life should come from God. He is to be our Example, Leader, and Guide in all that we do.** Our knowledge of God and His will comes as we read and study the revelation that He has given us in the Bible. In John 14:6 we read that Jesus said, *"...I am the way, the truth, and the life...."* Truth begins with God. God is Truth. God's Word is Truth (John 17:17). One of the reasons that God gave us His Word was to sanctify us. *"Sanctify them through thy truth: thy word is truth"* (John 17:17).

So, as Christians, we must realize that God is the basis of right and wrong and all we call moral. On the other hand, many in the world would tell us that there is no God. Others in the world would say that they believe there must be a God but that we have no way to know what He wants us to do or how He wants us to live and that He has left us to figure these things out for ourselves. These people tell us that right, wrong, and truth are "subjective"; that is, they must be determined by us, by our minds, consciences, and desires. They reason that since there is no God (or if there is a God, we can't know His mind), then each of us must decide for ourselves what is right, wrong, and true. This is why they argue that Christians should not tell them how to live or "make judgments about their *lifestyle.*" If there were no God, or if He had not made His will known in the Bible, they would be right. One individual would have no real authority to tell another what was right or wrong.

However, we know that God is real! We know He has given us His inspired Word and that He has preserved that Book. So we conclude that right, wrong, and truth are NOT determined by us or things within us. They are NOT subjective. **Right, wrong, and truth are <u>determined</u> by God!** So right, wrong, and truth are objective! The world teaches that right, wrong, and truth are subjective (determined in the mind of each individual), so they are relative. That is, it is up to each person to determine what is right or wrong. If two people have different opinions, something could be right for one and wrong for the other. And if there is no God or we can't know His thoughts, then "who is to say which is right and which is wrong?"

So, as Christians, we know right, wrong, and truth are objective, determined by God. When God says something is right, it is right for all. When God says it is wrong, it is wrong for all. When God says it is true, it is true for all. **That makes right, wrong, and truth ABSOLUTES!** We believe in absolute truth and absolute right and wrong.

Romans 3:3 says, *"What if some did not believe? shall their unbelief make the faith of God without effect?"* That is, if someone doesn't believe God's Word, does that make it untrue? If someone says, "I don't believe in hell," does that mean it doesn't exist? If someone says, "I don't think stealing is wrong," does that mean it isn't wrong? God answers in Romans 3:4, *"God forbid: yea, let*

God be true, but every man a liar...." That is, all that matters is what God says; what man thinks is irrelevant.

To the Christian, nothing is relative about right, wrong, or truth. They are absolute! That is, things that are right or wrong are right or wrong for everybody, everywhere, all the time. Things that are true are true for everybody, everywhere, all the time! They don't change with the situation, the time period, what everyone else is doing, or what everyone else thinks. They are absolute!

Sometimes while soul winning, after I present the Gospel or give my testimony, the person to whom I am speaking will say, "I am glad you found that to be true for you." The implication is that since they don't believe it, it isn't true for them. No! When a Christian dies, he is going to heaven. When a lost man dies, he does not go to heaven but will be in hell. Whether or not he believes it now, that is still the case. His unbelief doesn't change the truth. Someone may think he can defy the law of gravity, step off a five-story building, not fall, and not be hurt. But his opinion doesn't matter. Truth is objective and it is absolute. He will fall, and he will be hurt.

Right, wrong, and truth are absolute because they originate with the original—God. If you wanted to know if something weighed a pound, you would take it to your scale. Then if you had questions about the scale's accuracy and wanted to check it, you would compare it to a better scale. If you were still not satisfied, you would keep checking until you wound up at the Office of Weights and Measures, where you would compare the "pound" you had with the original kept in that vault. It is the original, and so all others must be compared to it.

SHOULD I?

Several times I have been to visit the National Archives Museum in Washington, D.C. There I have seen the original of the Declaration of Independence. It is the original. If someone had a copy but was not sure it was a correct copy, he could take that copy and compare it to the original there in that building.

The correct weight for a pound is determined not by someone's opinion, but by the original. The correct wording of the Declaration of Independence is not up to what someone thinks but is determined by comparing a copy to the original. So it is with right, wrong and truth. They are not determined by someone's subjective opinion; they are determined by comparing them to God, Who is the Truth and Who is right and holy (John 14:6; Leviticus 17:17)! One of the most important ideas we can teach to those we lead is that truth is absolute. Right and wrong are absolute. The moment anyone decides that truth, right, and wrong are subjective, based on opinion, or up to the situation—he is headed for destruction. Once he feels that it is up to him to determine right, wrong, and truth, he has no moorings and will justify anything!

As Christians, when we consider different matters, we must be careful that we do not fall into the mindset of the unsaved. When we begin with "I think" or "It seems to me," we are following the mindset that says right, wrong, and truth are subjective and determined by the individual. We must begin our reasoning with "God says…" or "Principles in God's Word teach…." My opinion does not matter; your opinion does not matter. What we must follow is God's opinion.

So our standards begin in the person of God. He is to be our example and guide. We should be holy because He is holy (Leviticus 11:44, 45). We should be pure because He is pure. We are to be truthful because He is the truth. We are to love others because He is love. These are the kinds of principles by which we should guide our lives. Then from these principles, God has given us standards or rules by which we should live so we can be God-like in our lives.

Seven Tests for Any Action

1. I don't want to disobey any Bible command.

2. I don't want to do anything that will develop an appetite that has no proper fulfillment.

3. I don't want to do anything that would impair my ability to serve God by weakening my health or diminishing my faculties.

4. I don't want to support financially those who are fighting God.

5. I don't want to be a friend of Satan instead of a friend of God.

6. I don't want to do anything that would have an appearance of evil.

   a. The Bible commands this.
   b. I don't want to hurt my testimony.
   c. I don't want to put myself in a position of temptation.
   d. I don't want to encourage others to sin.
   e. I want it to look like I love God and am on His side.
   f. The accusation of sin will hurt my ministry.
   g. The accusation of sin may hurt me legally.

7. I don't want to do anything that would go against my conscience.

CHAPTER THREE

THE PRINCIPLES OF SEPARATION

or
Seven Tests for Any Action

As Christians, we are often faced with questions about what would be the correct thing to do. As we saw in the chapter titled "The Foundation of Separation," we realize that what is right or wrong to do in any situation is determined by God—not by us. We realize that He has made us in His image, and we should live to glorify Him and to be like Him.

I believe the following guidelines will help us toward reaching that objective. I have taught this material for several years in Bible college and am listing these principles in the way I have taught them—as decisions I have made in my life. I call them "Seven Tests for Any Action."

1. I don't want to disobey any Bible command.

Clearly, this must be the beginning of our desire to do the will of God. Following this principle settles many of the decisions that we face in life. In Exodus 20, the Bible says, *"Thou shalt not commit adultery"* (v. 14). *"Thou shalt not steal"* (v. 15). These and so many other issues are settled if we simply obey the Word of God. In commands like these, God does not make exceptions.

27

He does not say they depend on the situation. A Bible command should settle any issue for a Christian. It doesn't matter how much the couple loves each other; adultery is wrong. It doesn't matter how needy I am or what I intend to do with the money; stealing is wrong. If you discuss any matter of right or wrong with the world, they will begin with "it just seems to me..." and then give a reasoned argument of why some sin should be permissible. However, if God says it is wrong, it is wrong for everybody—everywhere—all the time. I don't want to disobey any Bible command.

This also means that I must try to carry out all positive Bible commands. I must love my neighbor. I must try to witness to others. I must seek to obey every Bible command.

2. I don't want to do anything that will develop an appetite that has no proper fulfillment.

This decision is basic! Many of our appetites have to be fed or developed. As we feed appetites, they become stronger and stronger. At some point, some of these appetites can take over our lives. Very few, if any of us, were born wanting to eat broccoli. That was an appetite that had to be developed, and we developed it by eating small portions at first and then larger and larger portions. I have never heard of anyone who enjoyed smoking his first cigarette. The testimony of most, if not all, is that it made them sick. But they so wanted to be accepted by the world that they worked and worked at it until they developed an appetite for it, and then it led them to cancer.

If a couple sits for hours on a sofa, staring into each other's eyes, with their faces only inches apart, talking about how much they like each other, they are feeding appetites that have no proper fulfillment outside of marriage. So if they are not married, they are better off planning an activity they can appropriately enjoy together. In some cases (such as in the case of the couple), the appetites are not wrong in themselves, but the fulfillment of them at that time is wrong. The appetite has no proper fulfillment.

In some situations, some Christians will argue that a "little bit" of something is permissible and won't hurt you. "Just be careful you don't get carried away and do too much," they say. However, the wise Christian, the spiritual Christian realizes that in these situations (even if a little were okay), the "little bit" is giving him an appetite for more. He is feeding an appetite that has no proper fulfillment.

3. **I don't want to do anything that would impair my ability to serve God by weakening my health or diminishing my faculties.**

As a Christian, my objective in life is to glorify God and to serve Him by serving others. This was addressed in detail in chapter one. The only way I can serve God is in my body. I can serve him with my spirit, but that works through my body. I cannot tell someone the Gospel without a voice. I cannot write the Gospel without hands. I cannot read God's Word for myself or to others without eyes. I cannot hear preaching, except through my ears. I cannot lift up the fallen without the strength to do so. When we go soul winning, carry food to others, help clean the church, visit a bus route, or stand to preach, we do so in our body.

It is vital that I keep my body as well as possible so that I can serve God as long and as effectively as possible.

Because I serve God in my body, I must keep my mind sharp to avoid dangers and to have insight into situations and problems. I must not do anything that would diminish my faculties in any way. I want to be alert, healthy, and strong so that I can serve God (and others) as effectively as possible and so bring the most glory to God.

Several years ago, I was teaching along this line in Bible college, and I said, "I can't find a Bible verse that says I shouldn't poke out my eyes, but I'm not going to do so because it would ruin my quality of life and make me less able to serve God." I think the Holy Spirit put those words in my mind and voice. I did not have them in the notes and had never said them before. But that is the point here. Why are we so concerned with "prove to me it's wrong" instead of asking, "Will this help me to serve God better"? Many of the "questionable" practices about which Christians argue would not be an issue if this approach were taken.

4. **I don't want to support financially those who are fighting God.**

The money that I have is not really mine. It belongs to God. I am simply a steward or caretaker of it for God. That being the case, I want to use that money to bring glory to God. When I spend money on gasoline, food, or my electric bill, it is not going to Christians most of the time, but to a corporation that is generally neutral concerning Christianity. On the other hand, if I spent money at the liquor store or in the rock music industry or in many other areas, the money is going to those who are openly fighting against virtue, morality, and God.

Years ago, a store in the Hammond, Indiana, area had a large sign posted over the store reading, "Beer, Tobacco, Liquor," or something to that effect. I never went into the store but was told it also sold items such as ice cream and candy. Yet the emphasis of the store and what the owners advertised was beer, tobacco, and liquor. I would not have wanted to spend a nickel in that store as its goal was to promote what God is against.

5. I don't want to be a friend of Satan instead of a friend of God.

In I John 2:15-16 we read, *"Love not the world, neither the things that are in the world. If any man love the world, the love of the Father is not in him. For all that is in the world, the lust of the flesh, and the lust of the eyes, and the pride of life, is not of the Father, but is of the world."* James 4:4 says, *"... know ye not that the friendship of the world is enmity with God? whosoever therefore will be a friend of the world is the enemy of God."*

Most Christians are too in love with the world and too fascinated by the world. All of us must battle that affection from time to time. Many desire to be accepted by the world, to be approved by the world, and to have what the world has. Then we try to justify different actions so that we can be like them. I don't want to be like the world. I want to be like Christ. Dr. Jeff Fugate has said, "We're not out to impress the world; we're out to convert the world."

31

SHOULD I?

The world has nothing that can bring long-term joy or satisfaction. They have nothing worthwhile to offer to the Christian. Joy, satisfaction, and a blessed life come from serving God—not from trying to be like the world.

I have heard two Baptist preachers say they had an opportunity to witness to Elvis Presley, the "king" of rock 'n' roll. Both of these men said that Elvis gave them a clear testimony that, when he was young, he had trusted Christ as his Saviour. Whether he told them the truth, we do not know, but certainly he got away from the Christian life. He died August 16, 1977, at 42 years of age after years of drug abuse. He died in a mansion, but without friends, a wife, or people who cared. He reached the top of the world but had no joy or satisfaction.

I once heard Nancy Sinatra say on television that Elvis had told her, "Nancy, maybe I'd have been better off if I had just stayed in the church." And he would have! He would never have had his millions, but he would have had a satisfying life, probably a nice little home, a good family, and rewards in heaven! The world has nothing we should want!

6. **I don't want to do anything that would have an appearance of evil.**

Many years ago, when I was beginning to learn the Bible doctrine of separation, I did not understand this guideline. I was having a discussion with a Christian friend about whether or not something was acceptable for a Christian to do. My friend said, "Jim, even if what you were doing was okay, people would see you doing that and assume you were doing wrong things also."

I responded, "As long as I know I am doing right, what difference does it make what people think?"

My friend replied, "Jim, it makes all the difference in the world what people think. That is your testimony. That is your opportunity to minister."

I realized my friend was right and changed my attitude and actions on that day.

I want to spend more time on this point, not because it is the most important, but because many Christians fail to see its importance. Not disobeying a Bible command is the first criteria for an act, and that is obvious to all. The importance of appearance is debated by many Christians, and this principle is often not given its proper place. The Bible and common sense both teach that we need to be careful not only about what we do, but also about how it looks to others.

a. **Because the Bible commands this.** I Thessalonians 5:22 says, *"Abstain from all appearance of evil."* That command alone should settle it for a Christian. I should not appear to be doing wrong. I Timothy 3:7 requires that a pastor be of "good report." In other words, he must have a good name in the community. Proverbs 22:1 tells us that a *"good name is rather to be chosen than great riches."* Clearly, having a "good name" and being of "good report" deals with what people think about us. If my actions lead people to think I am stealing, dishonest, or immoral, I do not have a good name, nor am I of "good report." Romans 14:16 says, *"Let not then your good be evil spoken of."* In other words, we should do good in such a way that it appears we are doing good.

My good name is my reputation. It is not determined as much by what I do as by what people think I do. The Bible commands us to have a good name and to avoid the appearance of evil. The Bible says it **does matter** what people think!

b.   Because I don't want to hurt my testimony. My testimony is what people think of me and what they think I do. As my friend pointed out to me nearly 50 years ago, my testimony is my right to minister. My testimony helps me to help others. Since one of my goals as a Christian is to help others and since who comes to me for help will be determined by my testimony, I must keep my testimony clean. My testimony should validate all that I preach and all that I say in counseling. If people think I am dishonest, immoral, unjust or proud, they will not come to the church I pastor, the Sunday school class I teach, or ride the bus I captain. My opportunity to minister is going to be determined not only by what I do, but also by what I appear to do.

c.   Because I don't want to put myself in a position of temptation. Probably the best way to explain this truth is with an illustration. Suppose a young person who is a sincere Christian is invited by unsaved or rebellious friends to a party with drinking and drugs. He tells himself this would be a good opportunity to get to know these "friends" better so that he can eventually witness to them. So he decides to attend the party because he tells himself, "As long as I know when I leave that I didn't drink or do drugs, who cares what people think."

Unfortunately, if he goes to that party, people will assume that he has been drinking and/or doing drugs. That was the point of the party. Why else would anyone attend? He has put himself in a place with an appearance of evil. And in that place, he will be tempted to do wrong. He has put himself in a position where doing wrong is easy and where there will be temptation. He has made it more likely that he will do wrong.

This same truth could be illustrated by a situation where an unmarried couple spends hours alone in an apartment. They may say, "Nothing happened," and that may be the truth! But they will have a hard time convincing neighbors that is the case. They have put themselves in a situation with an "appearance of evil." And they have put themselves in a position of temptation.

In summary, if something has the appearance of evil, it is because it is a situation where most people in that situation would sin. So if I put myself in that situation, I will be tempted to sin, and it would be easy for me to sin. I want to avoid those situations because I want to avoid temptations, so that I can avoid sin!

d. Because I don't want to encourage others to sin. If I put myself in a position where it looks like I am sinning, others will think that it is okay to do what I am appearing to do, and they will be more likely to sin. The illustrations in the previous point would also apply here. If I, with a Christian testimony, am at the party with drinking and drugs, others will say, "I guess that isn't wrong. Even this Christian was doing it." That reasoning will make it more likely that they will sin. I want to keep others from sin, not encourage them to do it.

The same would apply to drinking what appears to be wine in a restaurant or buying wine for cooking. If others saw me sitting at the table or walking out of the store with a bottle of wine,

SHOULD I?

they would naturally think that I am doing what I appear to be doing. It would lead them to think "That must be acceptable."

e. **Because I want it to look like I love God and am on His side.** I was reared in Wisconsin in the 1950s and 60s. During that time, I became a serious Green Bay Packers fan. The team had great players including Starr, Taylor, Nitschke, Hornung, and many others, and they won several championships. I have attended very few Packers games because almost all of them are on a Sunday. A few years ago, the Packers had a pre-season game in and against Cincinnati on a Monday night. I decided to attend the game. When I went, I wore everything green and gold (the Packers colors) that I could find. I certainly would not have worn anything orange and black (Cincinnati's colors). I wanted it to appear to all that I was a Packers fan!

As a Christian, I want to **look** like a Christian and appear to be on God's side. It is a shame that many Christians care more about being identified with a sports team, than they do about being identified with God. Wherever I go and whatever I am doing, I want to look like a Christian. This will increase my opportunity to witness and decrease the chances of my being tempted to dishonor Christ. I certainly don't want it to **look** like I am following or promoting some rock star.

As a Packers fan in Cincinnati, I was in the minority. Our team (Green Bay) was away from home and just visiting. But I still wanted to make it clear where my loyalties were. As a Christian in this world, I am in the minority. I am away from home (heaven) and just visiting for a while. However, I still want to make it clear to all where my loyalties are!

f. **Because the accusation of sin will hurt my ministry.** As a Christian, I do not want to do anything that would cause me to forfeit my ministry. Certainly, if one is guilty of such an act, he should quietly resign. As a Christian leader, I also realize that if I am accused of something like that, it will hurt my ministry— even if I am totally innocent. The mere accusation will cause some to have doubts, others to leave, and many to have less confidence in me than they did before the accusation. So I want to live in such a way that such an accusation would be unlikely.

None of us can prevent anyone from just outright lying about us. In fact, the only protection any of us have from that kind of slander is the good faith of the rest of us. However, I want to live my life in such a way that if anyone ever would make such an accusation, people would say, "That doesn't sound like him. He is always so careful in that area." None of us want a testimony where people would say, "I have been wondering. It always seemed funny how he…"

If I have been avoiding all appearance of evil, I will have a good testimony, and the accusation will be less believable. That is, of course, if I have been concerned about not only what I do, but also how it looks. People will be more willing to give me the benefit of the doubt.

g. **Because the accusation of sin may hurt me legally.** The same principles apply in this point as in the last point. In some areas, if a child makes an accusation, the adult will be presumed guilty in the court of public opinion. And unfortunately and improperly, that will almost always be the case in the legal system. I want to live such a clean life with such a good name and testimony that no one would have the basis for such a lie, and I want to live so that if the lie were stated, no one would believe it.

7. **I don't want to do anything that would go against my conscience.**

The Bible clearly teaches that I should not do anything that would violate my conscience. That is, if doing it makes me feel guilty, then I shouldn't do it. Romans 14:23 says, *"...whatsoever is not of faith is sin."* That is, if I don't have the faith to believe that it is acceptable, then it is sin for me to do it. In the context, it is very clear that another may have faith to believe something is acceptable, and so to him it would be acceptable. However, if I do not have the same faith, it would be a sin for me because *"whatsoever is not of faith is sin."*

In I Corinthians 8:12, which is the center of a passage dealing with a weaker brother, Paul tells the Christians in Corinth that some of them might believe it was acceptable to eat the meat offered to idols. However, if a Christian who did not believe it was acceptable (had a weaker faith) ate, it would be sin for the weaker Christian. I Corinthians 8:12 says, *"But when ye sin so against the brethren, and wound their weak conscience, ye sin against Christ."* What wounds your conscience is a sin for you!

Paul stated in Acts 24:16, *"And herein do I exercise myself, to have always a conscience void of offence toward God, and toward men."* Paul's goal should be the goal of every Christian; we should work to have a clear conscience in all areas.

CHAPTER FOUR

DIFFERENCES IN SEPARATION

Before we begin a discussion of the applications of the principles of separation to the Christian life, I would like to address the reader who will not agree with some or with all the points of separation (standards) that are stated in the following pages. Certainly, good sincere Christians sometimes differ on a matter of separation. I have come to the standards stated in this book by personal study and am thoroughly convinced that all of them are the Biblical standard! However, I know that some sincere Christians will differ.

1. Respect those who differ.

The apostle Paul addressed these kinds of differences in Romans 14. I believe that God gives us the following principles in this chapter for dealing with Christians who have different convictions. First of all, we should respect them (Romans 14:1-12). *"Let not him that eateth despise him that eateth not; and let not him which eateth not judge him that eateth"* (v. 3). We are not to judge another because another Christian is not our servant, but God's servant. *"Who art thou that judgest another man's servant? To his own master he standeth or falleth"* (14:4a). However, because I am not to judge another Christian, this does not mean Biblical standards are not important. I must realize that *"we shall*

SHOULD I?

all stand before the judgment seat of Christ" (14:10), and *"every one of us shall give account of himself to God"* (14:12). And since I will stand before God and give an account of myself, I must be careful that I live my life with the purpose, goals, and standards that God has set forth in His Word. In summary, I should respect the one with different standards, but I must pursue the goals God has for me.

Secondly, regarding those with different standards, I should not try to weaken their convictions (Romans 14:13-20). In this passage, Paul had the faith to eat meat that another thought was improper. Paul commands his followers not to try to persuade others to abandon their stand against the meat. I have often repeated the statement that Dr. Jack Hyles made, "If you work as hard as I do to get people to have convictions, the last thing I want to do is try to talk anyone out of one." That is the Biblical approach taught in Romans 14:13-20.

Thirdly, God tells us in Romans 14:21-23 that if someone has more convictions than I do, then I should abide by his convictions while I am with him. Certainly, I don't want to encourage anyone to violate his conscience, nor do I want to weaken one of his convictions.

2. Don't spend too much time with those who differ—or they will influence you.

The people I am around, the sermons I hear, the music to which I listen, the books I read **will** have an effect on me! I have spent time with God, read HIS Book, listened to preachers, and

40

decided what I believe God's Word teaches. Since right, wrong, truth and falsehood are not determined by what I think, but by God, then I have closed the matter in my mind. God's Word teaches that it is wrong to drink alcohol. It does not matter what I think nor what those around me think. It is wrong! However, if I spend much time with social drinkers or with people drinking a beer or two while watching a football game on a Saturday, then drinking will become more acceptable in my mind. Their conduct and their convictions **will** influence me. This is why Lot's life was ruined while he lived in Sodom, why God wanted the Jews to kill **all** of the inhabitants of the land, and why God tells us to *"...come out from among them, and be ye separate"* (II Corinthians 6:17a).

Dr. Jack Hyles stated well, "I can decide who or what will influence me, but I cannot decide HOW it will influence me." It simply will not work to say, "I will study this compromiser and take the good." In the first place, you often can't tell the good from the bad. In the second place, even if you could make that distinction, you would still be influenced by everything he says, does, or writes.

I realized years ago that if I am around people, read their books, or attend their conferences, they **will** influence me. And the people and ideas that influence me **will** influence the people who follow me. So years ago I decided what I believe based on the Bible. Then I decided to spend time with others following the same path!

41

3. In summary

I should respect those who differ but not spend time fellow-shipping with them or studying them, or they will change me. I should spend my time with God and the Book He has written!

Recently, I was at a University of Kentucky basketball game. During the half-time break, I began chatting with the man sitting next to me. I try to at least give a tract or a word of testimony about the Saviour in those situations. As we talked, it became clear almost immediately that he was a Christian and, in fact, was also in the ministry. He told me he was on staff in a ministry that helped men start churches. He was working in the south-eastern United States and had helped to start several churches. I told him that our church was also very involved in starting churches. As we talked, it also became clear almost immediately that his was a liberal, modern approach with significantly different standards than our ministry. We were both pleasant toward each other, I enjoyed meeting him, and I believe he enjoyed the conversation also. I am glad for everyone who is saved or helped through his ministry. However, the Bible teaches that I should not fellowship with him nor work with him in the ministry. He and I will each answer directly to God at the judgment seat of Christ (Romans 14:10).

PART 2

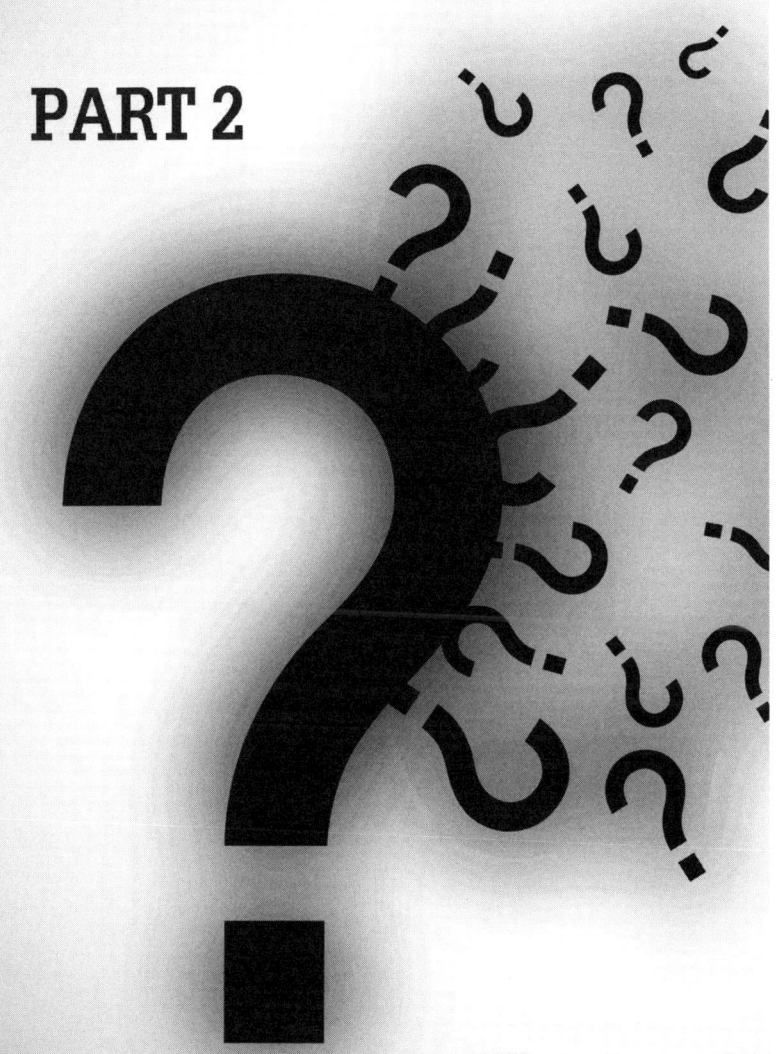

Applications of the
Principles of Separation

INTRODUCTION

As we begin a discussion of separation in personal standards, I would like to explain how I intend to deal with these matters. In this part of the book, I will apply the "Seven Tests for any Action" from Chapter 3 to different matters. Often I will refer to these directly, sometimes indirectly. In every area, I will begin with what I believe is a clear teaching of the Bible on the subject. In some areas, I will then deal with objections that some people raise to what I believe the Bible teaches. In most of these areas, I believe the Bible is very clear. In some, the Bible argument is not as strong, and I will try to explain why the course I have followed is what I believe God would prefer and why it seems best to me.

CHAPTER FIVE

THE CHRISTIAN AND ALCOHOL

Should a Christian drink alcoholic beverages in any form? The Bible clearly tells us that the answer to that question is "NO!" On this topic, we can simply go down the list of Seven Tests for Any Action and see that every one of them tells me I should not drink at all.

1. I don't want to disobey a Bible command.

The Bible tells us *"Look not thou upon the wine when it is red, when it giveth his colour in the cup, when it moveth itself aright"* (Proverbs 23:31). As we will see later in this chapter, the Bible uses the same word *wine* to describe all "fruit of the vine," whether it is fermented alcoholic wine or unfermented grape juice. Here in Proverbs 23, we are told not to even look at it when it *"moveth itself,"* which would be the bubbling action as the fermented alcoholic wine moves itself. Grape juice doesn't bubble and doesn't move itself. So if I am not supposed to even look at alcoholic wine, I shouldn't drink it.

Habakkuk 2:15a tells us, *"Woe unto him that giveth his neighbor drink."* So if I am not supposed to give it to others, clearly I should not drink it myself. If everyone followed this Bible command, there would be no alcohol to drink, as no one would give it to another.

Proverbs 20:1 states, *"Wine is a mocker, strong drink is raging: and whosoever is deceived thereby is not wise."*

Proverbs 23:20, 21 states, *"Be not among winebibbers; among riotous eaters of flesh: For the drunkard and the glutton shall come to poverty: and drowsiness shall clothe a man with rags."*

Proverbs 23:29, 30 states, *"Who hath woe? who hath sorrow? who hath contentions? who hath babbling? who hath wounds without cause? who hath redness of eyes? They that tarry long at the wine; they that go to seek mixed wine."*

2. **I don't want to develop an appetite that has no proper ful-fillment.**

The Bible has a myriad of verses that condemn drunkenness. It is true that there are fewer verses that totally condemn all drinking of alcohol. However, if you agree that drunkenness is condemned by the Bible, then it is clear that you should not drink *at all!* That is because if you drink even a little alcohol, you are developing an appetite that has no proper fulfillment, and that appetite could destroy you. I know that if I never develop a taste for beer by drinking just a "little bit" of it, then I will never consume many beers and be so drunk as to pass out. If I never sip a "little" wine at a fancy dinner, then I will never develop a taste for it that could cause me to wind up a wino. The end of the road for alcohol is poverty, homelessness, shame, and ruin. Why would anyone want to start down a path where the end is de-struction and say, "Don't worry, I'll stop before I get to the end"? The fact is, NO ONE who drinks a first beer or sips the first glass

48

of wine plans to arrive at the end of the road in destruction, BUT MANY DO WIND UP THERE. The way to be SURE not to arrive at that end is not to start on the road. Don't create the appetite that has no proper fulfillment by taking even the first drink!

Alcohol also gives the drinker an appetite for other sins. *"Thine eyes shall behold strange women, and thine heart shall utter perverse things"* (Proverbs 23:33). In Genesis 19, we have the story of Lot. His wicked daughters wanted him to "lie with them." They knew he would not commit such an abomination while sober, so they made him drunk. In Exodus 32:5, 6, God tells the story of the golden calf. After the people were drunk, they *"rose up to play"* in nudity and immorality.

3. **I don't want to do anything that will impair my abilities to serve God by weakening my health or diminishing my faculties.**

Everyone would agree that alcohol is not good for your health. That means I should not drink it at all. Certainly, the end of life for someone who is a steady drinker is poor health, cirrhosis of the liver, and an early grave. If someone is drunk, that person's judgment is clouded, his physical reactions are slowed, his inhibitions are lessened; he has given control of his body and life to alcohol. God commands us in Ephesians 5:18, *"Be not drunk with wine, wherein is excess; but be filled with the Spirit."* In both cases, the person yields control of his body to an outside influence. That influence will affect the person's speech, inhibitions, the way he walks, and give him boldness to say and do things he would never do on his own. As a Christian, that influence in my life must be the Holy Spirit, not alcohol.

Some may respond, "Yes, I realize that is true if I am drunk, but I will not get drunk. I will only drink a little." I maintain that anyone who drinks any alcohol is somewhat affected by it, and to that degree he is drunk.

> "When is a man drunk? When a man has drunk, he is drunk. Anybody who drinks beverage alcohol in any degree is somewhat affected by it, and so he is drunk to that degree. A man can get more drunk than he already is. He can drink until he is drunk, then he can drink until he is more drunk, then he can drink until he is unconscious and can't drink any more. A man can drink until a certain percentage of alcohol gets into the blood and stops the motor response so that he quits breathing and dies. Now, that is a little more drunk than he was while he was breathing. Yet he is drunk."[2]

Perhaps you would say, "It would take six beers for me to be drunk." And if you drink one beer, then you are one sixth drunk! You are one-sixth less able to serve God than you are before drinking.

I believe this is a good time to list the effects of alcoholic drink. Clearly, every one of these will make you less able to serve

---

[2]John R. Rice, *The Double Curse of Booze* (Murfreesboro: The Sword of the Lord Publishers, 1984), 3.

God. If you want to honor God and serve Him, you can't do it as well drinking alcohol!

According to the Word of God, the evil effects of strong drink fall into four separate categories: 1) the physical, 2) the mental, 3) the spiritual (moral), and 4) the material.

1. PHYSICAL
   a. Inflames the passions (Isaiah 5:ll)
   b. Inflames the eyes (Genesis 49:12; Proverbs 23:29)
   c. Leads to sickness (Hosea 7:5)
   d. Causes one to stagger (Job 12:25)
   e. Causes one to vomit (Isaiah 19:14)
   f. Weakens the vision (Isaiah 28:7; Proverbs 23:29)
   g. Leads one to wounds without cause (Proverbs 23:29)
   h. Produces filthiness (Isaiah 28:8)
   i. Produces giddiness (Proverbs 23:34)

2. MENTAL
   a. Impairs the judgment (Proverbs 31:5; Isaiah 28:7)
   b. Impairs the memory (Proverbs 31:4, 5)
   c. Infuriates the temper (Proverbs 20:1)
   d. Causes exhilaration (Genesis 43:34)

3. MORAL AND SPIRITUAL
   a. Leads to indifference for the work of the Lord (Isaiah 5:12)
   b. Is allied with gambling and licentiousness (Joel 3:3)
   c. Is allied with indecent exposure (Genesis 9:21; Habakkuk 2:15, 16)

4. MATERIAL (Prosperity and Happiness)
    a. Immediately
        1. Makes one oblivious to his misery (Proverbs 31:6, 7)
        2. Makes glad the heart (Psalm 104:15)
    b. Ultimately leads to:
        1. Ruin (Proverbs 23:32)
        2. Poverty (Proverbs 21:17; 23:21)
        3. Strife (Proverbs 23:29, 30)
        4. Woe and sorrow (Proverbs 23:29, 30)[3]

4. I don't want to support financially those who are fighting God.

The liquor crowd is clearly not the friend of God. I don't want to give ANY money to a group that is doing all they can to destroy the home, the church, and people's lives. This point really needs no further explanation.

5. I don't want to be a friend of Satan instead of a friend of God.

We are to be filled with the Holy Spirit, not the spirit of alcohol (Ephesians 5:18). Being filled with alcohol will lead me to do other things that will dishonor God, as we have already seen.

---

[3]Tom Wallace, *The Christian and Social Issues*, n.d., 7.

6. **I don't want to do anything that would have an appearance of evil.**

Even if someone would argue that it is not wrong to drink a little alcohol, this principle would make it clear that a sincere Christian should not drink at all. My little drinking would make it appear to others that it was okay to drink in general and would lead some to drunkenness. This principle means that I would not buy alcohol to use in cooking. Someone says, "When you cook it, the alcohol content is 'cooked out.'" Even if that is true, I wouldn't purchase the alcohol for cooking. Someone seeing me leaving the store with it would assume that I was drinking it, and they would be encouraged to do what I was appearing to do.

7. **I don't want to do anything that would go against my conscience.**

Drinking alcoholic beverages would certainly make me feel guilty, which means I shouldn't do it. Some might say, "Well, drinking doesn't hurt my conscience." That does not give you permission to drink. It simply gives you one less reason not to drink. You must avoid everything condemned by the Bible and everything that would give you a guilty conscience.

QUESTIONS PEOPLE ASK ABOUT ALCOHOL

As we begin this section, we should remember two basic principles of interpretation of the Bible or any other communication. First of all, you always interpret the unclear in light of the clear. Not every doctrine is fully explained in every verse of the Bible. But if you interpret the unclear verses in light of the clear passages, you will have no problem. Secondly, you always interpret the general in light of the specific. For example, the passage in John 2 where Jesus turned the water into wine is not written primarily to teach about alcohol. It is written to record His first public miracle. On the other hand, Habakkuk 2:15, Proverbs 20:1 and 23:31 are written about the dangers of alcoholic wine. So we interpret the general reference in John 2 in light of other specific references to this subject.

1. Didn't Jesus turn the water into wine?

Certainly in John 2:3-10, we are told that Jesus *"turned the water into wine."* However, in order to understand this passage of Scripture, we must understand that in the King James Bible, as well as in the Hebrew Old Testament and the Greek New Testament, there is only one word for the "fruit of the vine," and that word is *wine.* Sometimes it is clearly fermented (what we today call *wine,* with an alcoholic content). Sometimes it is not fermented and what we today call *grape juice,* with no alcoholic content.

You ask, how can you tell the difference? By the context. Many words have multiple meanings; we know which applies by the context. *Spring* can be "a season of the year," "a small stream," or "a piece of coiled wire." We know by the context which meaning applies. If someone says, "I am going fishing in the spring behind my house," no one wonders if the person is putting the fishing hook into the mattress that he discarded. The context makes it clear.

When the Bible says we shouldn't look at the wine when it *"moveth itself"* (Proverbs 23:31), clearly it is talking about the bubbling caused by fermentation. When the Bible says wine is a *"mocker,"* it is talking about fermented alcohol.

On the other hand, Mark 2:22 tells us, *"And no man putteth new wine into old bottles: else the new wine doth burst the bottles...."* Jesus used the word *wine* to refer to "unfermented grape juice" and emphasized that reference by calling it *new wine,* indicating it was freshly squeezed. There is a warning that if you put this new wine into containers that have already been stretched (old bottles), then when the grape juice ferments, the containers will not expand with it, and the contents will be lost. So it is clear Jesus knew the word wine sometimes described unfermented "fruit of the vine" and sometimes fermented "fruit of the vine." In order to avoid confusion, Jesus called the wine in this passage "new wine." Incidentally, the "bottles" in this passage were undoubtedly made of leather, as is explained in the definition of the word *bottle* in Webster's 1828 dictionary.

So we know that Jesus turned the water into *wine* and that this word refers sometimes to unfermented grape juice and sometimes to fermented alcohol. The context makes it clear that Jesus created grape juice. We know Jesus would not have given them alcohol that He condemns elsewhere in Scripture. Jesus would not have disobeyed the warning of Habakkuk 2:15, which says, *"Woe unto him that giveth his neighbor drink."* If he had disobeyed that warning, he would have had God's woe on His life and could not have died for our sins. Jesus would not have given them alcohol to lead to a drunken party with nakedness, lewdness, and immorality. Jesus would not have created anything that is decayed (and the fermentation in alcohol comes from decay). Obviously, Jesus did turn the water into the best grape juice they had ever tasted.

2.   **What about I Timothy 5:23? Did Paul tell Timothy to drink wine?**

This verse states, *"Drink no longer water, but use a little wine for thy stomach's sake and thine often infirmities."* There are two possible explanations to this verse. Neither of these explanations contradicts the Bible command against drinking alcohol. *Possibly, Paul is instructing Timothy to "use" some alcohol as a medicine.* Notice that Paul does not tell Timothy to drink the wine, but to "use" it. Certainly, the Bible does not condemn drugs for medicinal purposes that would otherwise be wrong to take. A person with extreme pain may take a drug to relieve that pain, when recreational use of the drug would be wrong. Until recently, the only drug commonly available was alcohol. It was used as pain killer during amputations during the Civil War. Now we have better drugs for that purpose. To "use" a drug as a medicine is not a problem. However, to drink alcohol as a beverage or to use any other drug for a "high" is wrong.

Secondly, Paul may have been recommending that Timothy drink some grape juice (non-alcoholic) for his upset stomach. Certainly, grape juice will have a calming effect on the stomach and will provide nutrients to the body. Drinking grape juice has often helped me when I didn't feel well.

Again, neither of these interpretations allow for the drinking of alcoholic wine as a beverage. Each of the explanations state a truth that is good, Biblical advice.

3.   What about Proverbs 31:3-9?

The general teaching of this passage clearly points out the problems caused by alcohol. Liquor will destroy the drinker by ruining judgment (v. 5), leading to adultery (v. 3) and taking away inhibitions (vv. 3-5). The passage is written to the leader, telling him to be sure to stand up for the poor and to judge righteously (vv. 8, 9), which he cannot do if he has been drinking (vv. 3-5), so he shouldn't drink. I think there are two possible interpretations of this passage, each of which teaches a Biblical truth. Perhaps the passage is saying in effect, "Let others ruin their lives with alcohol. God has called you to something better." H.A. Ironside's commentary states,

> Strong drink may help the despondent to forget their poverty and to remember their misery no more, but the true remedy is for the judge of the oppressed to hear their cause patiently and render a decision in righteousness, as he cannot do if under the power of wine.[4]

---

[4]H. A. Ironside, *Notes on the Book of Proverbs* (Neptune, N.J.: Loizeaux Brothers, 1908), 471.

SHOULD I?

The second possible explanation is that the passage may recommend alcohol as a drug, a sedative/pain reliever for a man in pain about ready to die or in misery. Sometimes someone has an incurable disease, is about "ready to perish," and we say, "They are just trying to make him comfortable now." That is certainly the proper thing to do in those situations. Someone may be hysterical because of a tragic event; a sedative for a brief time in that situation is appropriate. The only medicine available in Bible days was alcohol.

Wycliffe summarizes both of these explanations by saying the following:

> It may recommend alcohol as a drug. More likely,…regardless of others, you should not take it. Wine, women and song are the old debasing trio. A king has a higher responsibility.[5]

---

[5]Charles F. Pfeiffer and Everett F. Harrison, Eds., *The Wycliffe Bible Commentary* (Chicago:Moody Publishers, 1962), 582.

THE CHRISTIAN AND DRUGS

It seems appropriate to point out that any "recreational" use of drugs is wrong. If you consider the list of seven tests for any actions, any use of drugs is clearly banned by all of them. They will ruin your health, give you addictions, financially support Satan's crowd, ruin your home, and certainly make you less able to serve God.

You could re-read the chapter on alcohol and apply every point even more strongly to drug use. In addition to all of the points in that chapter, drugs are illegal. Christians are supposed to obey the law. Romans 13:1, *"Let every soul be subject unto the higher powers* [government]. *For there is no power but of God: the powers that be are ordained of God."* However, even if drugs become legal in the future, they are still off-limits for the Christian because of the Biblical principles already stated.

CHAPTER SEVEN

THE CHRISTIAN AND MUSIC

When it comes to this topic, I am certainly not a musician. While I have had some instruction in music, I am not an expert. On the other hand, I was reared in a moral Lutheran home in the 1960s; I attended a public high school with 2,000 students. Like almost everyone in the school, I listened to Elvis, the Beatles, and other similar groups, and I attended the dances. When I began to dedicate my life to serving God, I realized I had to turn away from that music if I wanted to be what God wanted me to be.

I will leave an explanation of the problems of rock music based on music theory to others who are much more qualified to explain it than I am. What I will give in this chapter are the reasons I knew rock music and other kinds of music were wrong. I believe the Biblical logic in these six points is clear and should be followed by all Christians who desire to be used of God. These are the reasons I use to select the kind of music to which I listen.

1.   Modern-day, secular, hard-rock music is wrong.

This point seems very clear to me. The hard-rock music of today is many steps worse than the songs of the 50s and 60s. That older music is so-called "classic rock," and while it is still wrong, it is nowhere near as bad as the hard-rock music of today.

a. Much of today's hard-rock music contains vulgar and immoral lyrics. While waiting in lines in electronic and appliance retail stores, I have heard rock songs with lyrics describing the most intimate of husband-wife relations. Such language is clearly a violation of Scripture.

b. Many of the lyrics in these songs are anti-God. They defame God, taunt Him, joke about His existence, etc. Clearly a Christian should not listen to that kind of music.

c. Many of the modern-day, hard-rock musicians use their fame to promote Satan worship, immorality, the occult, drugs, anarchy, new-age religions, and other beliefs and acts that are clearly anti-Bible and anti-God.

d. The money made in this industry is used to promote and support everything that God is against. And the money made in this industry is used to attack everything God is for. If I am going to be a good steward of the money God has entrusted to my care, I can't spend any money on rock music.

e. The beat in rock music makes you want to dance in vulgar, suggestive motions. I will spend more time in the next chapter explaining why a Christian should not dance. Here, I want to simply talk about the rock beat as it relates to dancing. I cannot explain it with music theory, but I do know from my high school days that rock music has a "danceable beat." It encourages you to dance. Other songs may be lively and peppy, but the beat just isn't in the right place if you were to try to dance to it. "Jingle Bells" is a lively, peppy song, but the beat is different than the beat to even the old rock songs like "Jailhouse Rock" or "Rock Around the Clock." You can't dance to "Jingle Bells," but you are encouraged to dance to the others. A dedicated Christian should not listen to any music that encourages dancing because, as we shall see in the next chapter, dancing is wrong.

I do not know any Christian who would defend the kind of music I have described in this section as acceptable. Certainly, some Christians would argue that Christian rock is acceptable, but even those believers would agree that the kind of music I have described above is wrong. So, I think we can all agree here that "modern-day, secular, hard-rock music is wrong."

2.   "Christian rock" music is wrong.

Anyone who wants to be a holy (separated) Christian should not listen to music that has the rock beat—even if it has Christian words.

   a.   "Christian rock" music is wrong because it develops an appetite for secular rock music. This is an application of the second of the general principles from Part I of this book. This principle became clear to me in my personal life because of the area of music. Because I grew up listening to Elvis, the Beatles, etc., I developed an appetite for that music. When I was about 20 years old, I realized it was wrong, and I quit listening to it. However, I had developed an appetite for it, and I would still enjoy listening to it. That appetite has never left me. On the other hand, I quit listening to rock music before the heavy metal sounds became popular. I have never listened to that music, never developed an appetite for it, and

63

have never enjoyed it. Heavy metal music sounds, to me, like clashing and clanging. I do not enjoy it, and because I never developed an appetite for this kind of music, it presents no real temptation to me.

A Christian who listens to "Christian rock" music will develop an appetite for that sound. When he searches for music on a car radio or an Internet site, he will select music with that same sound, which will take him to the modern-day, secular, hard-rock music.

b. "Christian rock" music is wrong because it is an attempt to appeal to the world by being like the world. But that is not God's method. We are to be separated unto God—not like the world. The Christian is to appeal to the world by being God-like and offering an alternative to the world.

c. The beat in any rock music (Christian or secular) encourages dancing. And as we will see in the next chapter, that is not appropriate for a Christian.

For these reasons, I decided that I should not listen to "Christian rock" music. It is not appropriate for the child of God.

3. **A large percentage of "country music" is wrong.**

I would agree that some country songs contain acceptable lyrics. Some of the lyrics talk of God, mother, our country, and virtues in a good light. It is also true that some of the songs on a country station would have a beat that is not sinful. On the other hand, MANY of the lyrics to country songs promote drinking, divorce, cursing, immorality, and other unbiblical activities and philosophies. If you develop an appetite for country music, you will be listening to the country stations and, therefore, listening to these unbiblical philosophies being promoted. And when you hear them promoted again and again, you will begin to lose your aversion and hatred toward these activities. You will not be able to "just listen to the OKAY country songs." You will hear them all, and MANY of the lyrics will cause you to lose your hatred of sin and fear of it.

Secondly, the beat in many country songs is the same kind of beat as in rock music. It encourages dancing. It develops an appetite for that kind of beat, and a Christian should not listen to it.

4. **As a Christian, I shouldn't listen to any music that develops an appetite for any music that is wrong.**

5. **Regarding Christian "quartet" music—if it has a wrong (danceable) beat, I won't listen to it.**

This music is developing an appetite for what is wrong and is encouraging dancing.

6. **If a group has a significant percentage of their music that is wrong for any reason, then I won't listen to the group or own their CDs.**

This would include many of the modern Christian quartet groups—if very much or all of their music has that danceable beat. It would include nearly all country musicians. I simply do not want to get into something that has the potential of taking me away from God. This kind of music does not draw a person toward God; rather, it pulls the person away from Him. I have heard a recording of Elvis Presley singing "Amazing Grace." He has a beautiful voice. He probably "slides" his notes more than someone should. But it is certainly not rock music, the words are tremendous, and it is not a rock beat. However, I would not choose to listen to the Elvis rendition of "Amazing Grace," and I certainly would not buy it because I don't want to be associated with everything else Elvis represents. I don't want to be tempted to try to find another song of his that is not "very wrong" and thus begin my slide toward sin.

CONCLUSION

In Part I of this book, I stated a thought that I believe the Holy Spirit gave me as I was teaching Biblical Separation in a college classroom. "I can't find a Bible verse that says I shouldn't poke out my eyes, but I am not going to do so because it would ruin my quality of life and make me less able to serve God." Why don't we stop saying, "Prove to me it's wrong!" Why don't we start asking, "Will this help me to serve God better and accomplish more for Him?"

CHAPTER EIGHT

THE CHRISTIAN AND DANCING

What about dancing for the Christian? I will consider two kinds of dancing. The first is what we will call "slow dancing," where you hold your partner and move to a slow beat. The other is what we will call "fast dancing," where the music is much faster and you do not hold your partner.

Concerning slow dancing, the dancers are hugging someone who is not their husband or wife, holding their bodies together, and moving with the music. Clearly, this is not appropriate for the Christian young person who should keep his or her body for his or her future mate. Nor is it appropriate for a Christian married person to be holding another person in that manner. The physical contact in the "slow dance" is not wholesome. It will lead to other desires and often to improper actions.

Concerning modern fast dancing, most of the movements are sensual. The movements in fast dancing highlight parts of the body that are personal, and they do it with suggestive movements. Fast dancing is meant to be suggestive and enticing. While a young lady may not be thinking that way while she is dancing, many of the people watching her are. In addition to this aspect of fast dancing, a person cannot dance this way without listening to rock music, and the problems with rock music have already been addressed in the previous chapter.

I have been working with Bible college students for many

years. Occasionally, girls have asked, "What about dancing with your father or husband at your wedding?"

Since I feel that Bible principles teach that dancing in general is wrong, I do not think it would be wise for a person to dance in a specific case that he/she might argue is permissible. Certainly, a husband and wife should hug and hold each other. On the other hand, for a bride and groom to dance at their wedding would hurt their testimony. Others will automatically assume that the couple dances in general, and they will be encouraged to dance in general.

A couple's wedding day should be one of the highlights of their life. It should be planned to glorify God and show their dedication to serve Him as a couple. To dance at the reception would not show that dedication.

CHAPTER NINE

THE CHRISTIAN AND GAMBLING

It seems clear to me that Bible principles teach that a Christian should not gamble in any form or for any amount. While I cannot quote a Bible verse that teaches all gambling is wrong, the principles stated in Part I of this book are clearly against gambling. Let us remind ourselves again that our purpose in life is to glorify God and serve Him by serving others. I want to include things in my life that will help me to do that, and I want to avoid anything that will hinder me (or that might hinder me) in that goal.

As I have already stated, I cannot find a Bible verse that tells me not to poke out my eyes, but I am not going to do it because it would hinder my quality of life and make me less able to serve God. The same can be said for gambling. The following principles will apply to this practice.

In the first place, God's plan is that each of us work to meet our needs and get money. II Thessalonians 3:10b says, *"If any would not work, neither should he eat."* This verse and many others teach that principle. If I gamble, the only way for me to get money is for someone else to lose it. So I am trying to get money from another without working for it or earning it. I am hoping to "trick" him out of his money. That reasoning is close to stealing. The Bible teaches that I should earn money by *labor*—"providing goods or services."

69

Secondly, we should remember that all we have belongs to God. The money I have with which I could gamble is not my money; it is God's money. When anyone gambles, he is not being a good steward of the things God has entrusted to his care.

All gambling odds are set up so that the "house" (the people who own the casino or run the lottery) will keep a significant percentage of the money. If people gamble long enough, they may "win" occasionally, but eventually they will lose their money to the people running the operation. If you gave a friend $10 to keep for you while you played basketball, then came back to get your money later and found he had purchased lottery tickets with it (that the "odds are" would lose), you would be upset. God feels the same way about the money He entrusts to us—if we gamble it away.

Thirdly, let me remind you of the fourth principle mentioned in the tests for any action. "I don't want to support financially those who are fighting God." When you gamble, your money eventually winds up flowing to the "house," that is the people running the operation. And the casino owners are not God's people. They are fighting God.

Fourthly, gambling associates me with the wrong crowd. Joel 3:3 says, *"And they have cast lots* [gambled] *for my people; and have given a boy for an harlot, and sold a girl for wine, that they might drink."* Gambling will take you to the casinos, which are places where people also go to drink alcohol and watch lewd shows, both of which lead to immorality.

Fifthly, and maybe the most important reason to avoid gambling is the principle that "I do not want to develop an ap-

petite that has no proper fulfillment." In a sermon, I mentioned that Christians should not gamble. After the service, a new Christian came to me and talked to me about gambling.

He asked, "Not even a two-dollar lottery ticket?"

I explained some of the things that I stated earlier in this chapter and then added that one might argue, "It is only $2; I can afford to lose it. I'll just spend it on a lottery ticket every week instead of a cup of coffee." And on the surface, that sounds harmless. But oftentimes that small bet becomes a larger bet. The thought becomes "The jackpot is bigger this week, so I'll buy extra tickets." Then after a while, the extra tickets become the norm.

The problem is that none of us know if we will stop with one ticket or if gambling will become something that consumes us. Certainly, when anyone buys a single ticket, he is feeding an appetite (of hoping to win the jackpot) that can lead him to spend the grocery money or the rent money on lottery tickets. That appetite has no proper fulfillment.

Even if the appetite for winning the jackpot does not consume you and you don't go into poverty because of gambling, you have to consider the example you are setting for your family and others. I mentioned to that new Christian with whom I was talking, "Even if you never go beyond one ticket a week, suppose your son follows your example and starts buying one ticket a week, but it does consume him. He winds up in poverty because of a gambling habit that started when he followed your one-ticket-a-week example."

No Christian should gamble in any form or for any amount.

Should I?

Gambling is not being a good steward, it is associating yourself with the wrong crowd, it is feeding an appetite that has no proper fulfillment, and it is encouraging others to go a step beyond where you have gone.

Because I do not want to gamble or encourage others to gamble, I believe I should separate from places and practices that are associated with gambling or that overtly encourage gambling. One such thing would be the standard deck of playing cards. Because the principle and primary association of a deck of cards is gambling, I will not play any games with them, nor will I have them in my home.

I now live in Lexington, Kentucky, which is called "the horse capital of the world." What is meant by that nickname is "the horse racing capital of the world" since more thoroughbred race horses are bred in this area than anywhere else. However, I would not attend a horse race because the principal activity at the horse race is betting. If you watch the shows leading up to the Kentucky Derby or any other horse race, the commentary is focused on the betting odds for each horse. While you can bet on anything, the emphasis at a horse race is on the betting. If you watch the pre game show for a football game, the commentary is on the match ups and the game plans. Horse racing focuses on gambling, while football focuses on football.

Before I leave the topic of gambling, let me say a word about investing. Sometimes as I have taught this material in Bible college, students will ask, "What about investing in stocks? Isn't that gambling?"

I do not believe they are the same thing at all. When someone starts a business, he invests his time, his money, and other people's money into that business. He plans to produce goods or provide services that others need. He expects to be paid for the value of what he produces. He expects, through hard work and wise decisions, to make a profit on his investment. If a third party also invests in that business, he expects that the money he provides will enable the entrepreneur to do a better job of producing goods and services that will have value, so that they will both make a profit. When someone buys a stock, he becomes a part owner of the company. He expects that as the company continues to provide goods and services of value, he will receive a share of the profits (dividends) and that the stock will increase in value.

Certainly, in all investments there is a risk. But making an investment that has a risk is NOT the same thing as gambling. When I make an investment, I expect to earn a profit based on the work done by the company to produce goods and services. The money that I receive from others is based on work. When someone gambles, he hopes to receive money from others based on chance and without doing any work.

All investments have risks. If you buy a home, you have an investment that you hope will increase in value based on your wise selection of the home, neighborhood, and your work to maintain the home, but there is no guarantee; there is risk. However, when you buy a lottery ticket, you hope to win the jackpot without any work.

Even the money invested in savings accounts has some risk (as many from the Depression era will testify). And if you bury the money in your backyard, there is the risk that it will be stolen and the risk that it will lose its value due to inflation. There is a difference between a risk and gambling.

CHAPTER TEN

THE CHRISTIAN
AND APPEARANCE

There is probably no area that causes more problems for fundamental pastors and no issue that causes more people to leave fundamental churches for more "progressive," less restrictive churches than the issue of appearance. In over forty years of Bible college work, I have found that it takes a constant vigil to monitor the standards of the students in this area. Probably in some cases, improper attire is due to carelessness or a lack of instruction. In other cases, it is intentional.

This chapter will be divided into several sections—each of which will give Bible teaching concerning different aspects of the Christian's appearance. It is my prayer that you will read these pages with a heart that says, "I want my appearance to be what God would want it to be."

CONCERNING MODESTY

Certainly the Christian lady and the Christian man should dress modestly. The Bible is very clear on that topic. While some may have differing opinions on what is modest, it would surely seem that every sincere Christian would agree that he or she should dress modestly. *A good summary would be that your clothing should be modest and not call attention to itself or to your body.* The following principles on this topic are clearly stated in the Word of God.

a.   It is wrong for a person to expose or attire his or her body so as to emphasize sex appeal. I Timothy 2:9 says, *"In like manner also, that women adorn themselves in modest apparel, with shamefacedness and sobriety...."* All Christian men (and women) should be clothed in *modest apparel.*

b.   There is such a thing as the *"attire of a harlot."* Proverbs 7:10, *"...there met him a woman with the attire of an harlot...."* This clothing is intended to provoke the desires of the opposite gender and should not be worn by any Christian. If a garment displays the body the way a harlot would display her body, the Christian should not wear it. Some clothing is just wrong.

c.   The Bible teaches that a man should not look at a woman and lust after her. Matthew 5:27, 28, *"Ye have heard that it was said by them of old time, Thou shalt not commit adultery: But I say unto you, That whosoever looketh on a woman to lust after her hath committed adultery with her already in his heart."*

d.   A woman is not to dress so as to tempt the man to lust after her. If she does dress that way, she is a participant in the sin. Matthew 5:28 says that he commits adultery *"with her"* in his heart.

e.   As a general rule, a Christian's clothing should be modest and not call attention to itself or to the body. If your clothing emphasizes the curves of the body, it is wrong. Your clothing should hang loosely. If your clothing exposes or nearly exposes any private areas of the body, it is wrong. If your clothing is sheer enough, tight enough, low enough, or short enough to say "Look here," then the clothing is wrong. I Peter 3:3-6 talks to ladies and says,

> *"Whose adorning let it not be that outward adorning of plaiting the hair, and of wearing of gold, or of putting on of apparel; But let it be the hidden man of the heart, in that which is not corruptible, even the ornament of a meek and quiet spirit, which is in the sight of God of great price. For after this manner in the old time the holy women also, who trusted in God, adorned them-selves, being in subjection unto their own husbands: Even as Sara obeyed Abraham, calling him lord: whose daughters ye are, as long as ye do well, and are not afraid with any amazement."*

Certainly, the Bible does not teach against wearing gold or fixing your hair. If that were the teaching, then it would also teach not to wear clothes. What God is teaching is that your attractiveness should not be found in your clothes or appearance, but in your spirit! People should be impressed with your spirit, not with your clothes, makeup, or physical attributes.

CONCERNING PANTS FOR WOMEN

There is probably no topic as controversial in fundamentalism as the wearing of pants by women, and no standard that is deteriorating as rapidly. The more I study this issue, the more I am convinced that it is improper for a woman to wear pants.

Should I?

Deuteronomy 22:5 says, "*The woman shall not wear that which pertaineth unto a man, neither shall a man put on a woman's garment: for all that do so are abomination unto the LORD thy God.*" Several different aspects of this verse will be addressed, but let me begin by pointing out that *the verse clearly states* that *some clothes are for women and other clothes are for men.* It is also clear that when God gave this verse to Moses, *God did not want men and women wearing each other's garments.* That leaves us with two questions that need to be answered:

1) Does God feel the same about people wearing garments for the opposite gender today as He did when He told Moses that such a practice was an abomination?

2) What garments are for men, and what garments are for women?

Some have tried to dismiss this verse by arguing that in the Bible time everyone wore robes, and men and women dressed alike. Obviously, that is NOT the case. When God gave Moses the words to Deuteronomy 22:5, some garments were men's garments, and others were for women, or the verse makes no sense at all. God, through Moses, could not have said "*the woman shall not wear that which pertaineth unto a man*" if both men and women wore the same clothes at that time. Obviously, some clothes were for men and others were for women when that Scripture was written.

So we must begin by asking if God has changed His mind about men and women wearing each other's garments. I believe the answer to this is a very clear "NO, He has not changed His mind." In his book, *Preaching Standards: Right or Wrong?* Dr.

Mike Allison does a thorough study of the use of the word *abomination* in Deuteronomy 22:5. He points out that the word is used only of things that are a sin at all times.[6] The word *abomination* is never used of things like plowing with different animals yoked together nor of sowing divers seeds. God carefully makes it clear that wearing each other's garments is an abomination (and a sin at all times).

God made Adam and Eve male and female. He made them different physically. From the very beginning, He gave them different roles in life. God is not for obliterating the distinctions between the genders; He is not for the "unisex" movement. He is also not for obliterating the distinctions in attire for men and women.

I believe nearly all Christians would agree that God has not changed His mind about men and women wearing each other's clothing. For a man to wear a dress or other "female" clothing would be called "cross-dressing" and considered wrong. It is just as wrong for a woman to wear a man's garment.

So we come to the second question, "What garments are for men, and what garments are for women?" That is, we must examine what the attire of a man is and what the attire of a woman is.

We must look for Bible answers to these questions and not simply look to today's society or the fashion designers of our day. We must ask, "Has God expressed an opinion?" The world may say that it is acceptable for women to wear pants, but that

---

[6]Mike Allison, *Preaching Standards: Right or Wrong?* (Shelbyville, Tenn.: Bible and Literature Missionary Foundation, 1984), 3-14.

does not make it acceptable in God's eyes. The world also says that a couple living together before marriage is acceptable, that homosexuality is acceptable, and that parading your body in a skimpy bikini is acceptable, but that does not make it so.

The Old Testament laws express God's views on many topics. If we want to know God's mind on something, we should ask ourselves, "What has He said about it?" While I understand that Deuteronomy is in the Old Testament and we are living in New Testament times today, we are still supposed to follow God's desires in all that we do, including what we wear. So as I look for guidance on what God wants me to do, it seems clear He still doesn't want us to do things that He said were an abomination years ago. The *"attire of an harlot"* is Old Testament also, but it is still wrong for a New Testament Christian.

When we study the Bible, we see that pants are a masculine garment, designed to be worn by men. They were worn only by men in Bible times. Long flowing robes, which would be similar to dresses of our day, were worn by women.

The Bible does not often go into great detail in describing the clothing to be worn. The word *breeches* ("britches") appears five times in the Bible. In each case, it is describing what we would call pants, and in each case, they are part of a detailed description of clothing for the priest, who was always a man. Men in Bible times wore robes (mantles) over their "breeches." Then when it was time to work or to go to war, they would "gird up" their robe (tuck it into the *girdle* or sash that they wore around their waist) so they could be active. They were still modestly covered by their breeches. Women were not commanded to gird up their robes because they were not wearing breeches with the robe. They had a longer, flowing robe, more like a dress.

So we conclude that the Bible teaches that pants (breeches) are for men, and dresses (long flowing robes) are for women. Pastor Jeff Fugate has often said, "I just don't see any exceptions in that verse."

Another reason for women not to wear pants is that of modesty. Certainly in pants, a woman's form, the shape of her body, is displayed. This is not the case in an appropriate dress. Someone may say, "A woman can't play some sports or engage in certain activities with modesty in a dress." But I know of nothing in the Bible that commands her to participate in these activities; however, she is commanded not to dress like a man. She is commanded to be modest.

I had a college student write in a paper, "I am to be modest, so I cannot participate in activities that would cause me to be immodest."

Some Christians would reply, "But I enjoy that activity."

As a matter of fact, even most sin is enjoyable (briefly), but that does not mean it is acceptable. If someone cannot participate in an activity while being modest, she (or he) should not participate!

Some would say, "I enjoy lying on a beach in a bikini."

But enjoyment does not make it right.

Some may say, "I enjoy getting drunk" or "I enjoy committing adultery," but these actions are still sins.

Simply because you enjoy an activity does not mean that it is what God would want you to do. Once again, since God has commanded us to be modest, we must refrain from activities that would require us to be immodest.

In conclusion, I believe the Bible teaches that a lady should not wear pants 1) because the Bible commands her not to do so, 2) because they are not modest, and 3) because doing so is one more step in breaking down the distinctions between the genders—and God is opposed to the "unisex" movement.

Concerning "Faddish" Clothes

As explained at the beginning of this chapter, I believe the Bible teaches that a Christian should dress neatly, modestly, and attractively. Our clothes should not "make a statement" or call attention to us. I Peter 3:2-6 and other Scriptures are clear on this matter. With that in mind, I think it is unwise for a Christian to wear trendy, mod clothing. If your clothes would cause someone to say, "Look at that outfit; it's really unusual," then I think that is not best for a Christian. Often "faddish" clothes seem to say, "I don't want to look like a Christian." However, I DO want to look like a Christian.

I have already discussed this subject at some length in chapter 3 under the heading of avoiding appearance of evil. Just like I wanted to look like a Green Bay Packers fan while attending their game in Cincinnati, I want to look like a Christian while living on this earth.

Some fashions, makeup or hairstyles have been made popular by ungodly musicians, Hollywood actors, or entertainers. To have that "look" about you would automatically identify you with them. People would see you and say, "Oh, he is a follower of __."

Certainly, I do NOT want that thought of me, so I would not dress in that manner.

For over 35 years, I have visited on bus routes in some of the most crime-filled areas near the places I have lived. When I visit in these areas, I wear a collared shirt and a tie. I have had people tell me as I visited that they thought I was a preacher or a detective or a lawyer. In all of these years, I have never been approached to buy drugs or with any other illicit offers. I believe the reason I have been spared from that is my appearance. I want to continue to look like a Christian!

CONCERNING MIXED SWIMMING

Since the Bible commands us to be modest (I Timothy 2:9; I Peter 3:2-6 and other passages), the Christian cannot participate in this activity. Even the world will dress more conservatively with street clothes or robes while going to and from the pool or the beach because they realize they are immodest. Somehow, they (and many Christians) excuse their extreme lack of clothing by saying, "It's okay because we are near water (swimming)." But that excuse does not make mixed swimming acceptable to God.

In addition to the basic (and obvious) modesty issue, Dr. John R. Rice has said, "For a person to expose their body in swimsuits does not encourage them to save their body for their spouse." I believe he was correct.

CONCERNING HAIR LENGTH

The Bible teaches very clearly that a man should have short

hair and a woman should have long hair. *"Doth not even nature itself teach you, that, if a man have long hair, it is a shame unto him? But if a woman have long hair, it is a glory to her: for her hair is given her for a covering"* (I Corinthians 11:14, 15). That passage teaches that a woman is to wear long hair as a symbol of her submission to God and to her husband. Someone will ask, "What is short?" The answer is that "short" is the opposite of "long." So if your hair is long, it is not short. If your hair is short, it is not long.

CHAPTER ELEVEN

THE CHRISTIAN AND MOVIES

In general, the movie industry today promotes just about everything that God's Word says is wrong, and that same movie industry criticizes just about everything that God's Word says is right. The movie industry is opposite of God on just about everything. Movies, in general, do not promote good; they are produced by the unsaved, anti-God crowd. Watching movies is not going to draw you to God but will pull you away from God.

I would not want to spend money to go to the movie theater, purchase DVDs or download movies over the Internet. I believe that money spent that way is supporting Satan's crowd—the crowd that is actively attacking God—and goes against the fourth principle that was given in chapter 3 of this book. Dr. Jeff Fugate has said, "When you support movies, you are supporting the place that attacks home, church, America, modesty, and decency."

Most movies include bad language or cursing or indecency or unbiblical teachings about false gods or several of these things. They will draw you away from God, not bring you closer to God. In general, movies produced by the movie industry feed the flesh.

It seems to me that with the development of television, cable television, and the Internet, drawing a clear line on right and wrong on movies has become more and more difficult. The medium itself is not sinful. A home movie or a video of a Christian event, play, or sermon posted on the Internet or distributed on a DVD is not wrong. It seems to me that even a thirty-minute television show such as *The Andy Griffith Show* is basically a thirty-minute movie (usually presented with an appropriate theme and a good lesson).

That being stated, it is still clear that the movie industry—what we call Hollywood—is basically anti-God, anti-church and anti-decency. The industry is for everything I oppose and against everything I believe is right. When Christians can quote long passages of movies, it seems clear to me that they are spending too much time watching movies and not enough time in the Word of God.

· It is also true that movie theaters are generally places of improper conduct between couples. If you attend a movie on a date, people will assume you were inappropriate. That assumption will hurt your testimony. If you promote movies by attending them or by talking about them, you are hurting your testimony and encouraging other people to delve into something that can only hurt them. Occasionally, I have heard preachers take sermon illustrations from movies. I think this is very unwise; that preacher is promoting activities that can only hurt his people.

Probably there are some gray areas in this matter. Again, the idea of a video or a moving picture is not wrong. However, the "movie industry" is wrong on just about everything. As Christians, it behooves all of us to be separated from the "Hollywood crowd." Rather than thinking "If *A* is acceptable, then surely *B* is permissible," instead we should think, "If there is sin or danger in *B* and *A* is somewhat like "*B*," then I should also avoid "*A*."

In over forty-five years of ministry, most of it working with

Bible college students, I do not know of any person whose life was hurt because he stayed too far away from movies. However, I know of many who were led out of God's path into the world by being too involved with movies.

PART 3

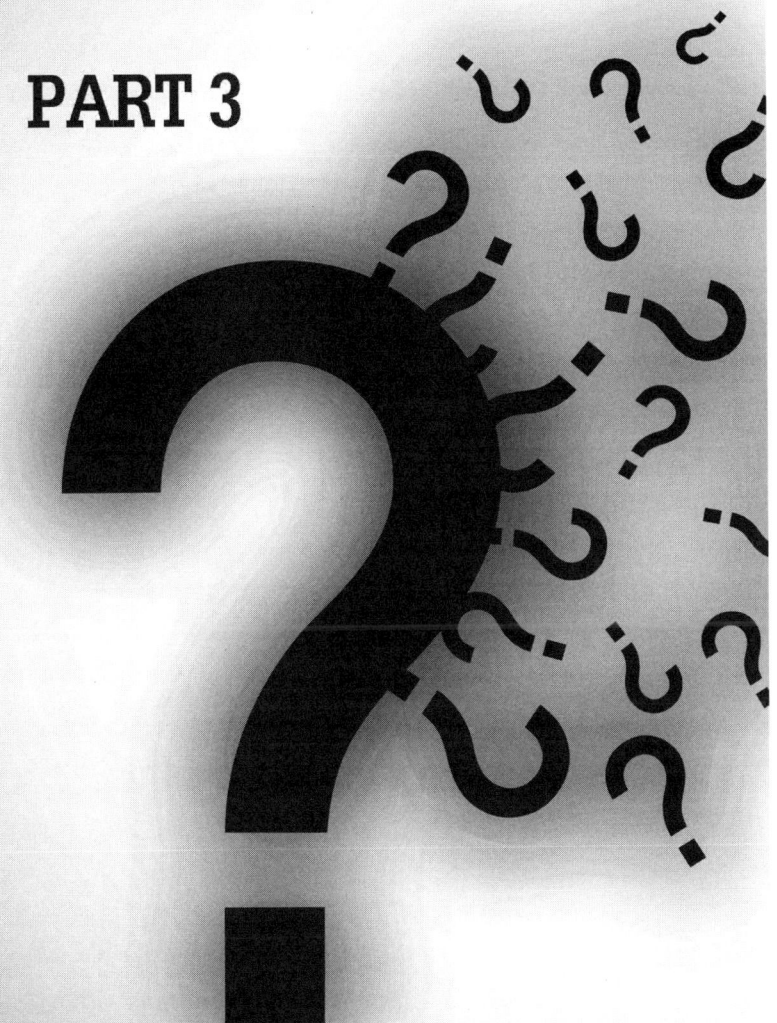

Concluding
Thoughts

CHAPTER TWELVE

CONCLUSION

God has saved us to glorify Him. We should seek to separate from any thing, any practice, or any one who would hinder us in fulfilling that purpose for our lives. The purpose of separation is so that we can accomplish what God wants us to accomplish.

Some will say, "You are a legalist." Let me point out that EVERYONE has things that he thinks are wrong to do. Even the unsaved liberal has some things that he thinks are wrong to do. So if saying something is wrong makes you a legalist, then EVERYONE is a legalist. Usually, someone calls you (or me) a legalist when you (or I) point out that the Bible teaches it is wrong to do something that he enjoys doing.

The words *legal, legalist,* and *legalism* are not in the King James Bible. In a theological sense, a *legalist* is usually described as "someone who adds works to grace for salvation." Doing this makes the Gospel into another gospel (of a different kind)—and perverts the Gospel. However, just because I can be saved without works doesn't mean that I should not do good works.

"For by grace are ye saved through faith; and that not of yourselves: it is the gift of God: Not of works, lest any man should boast. For we are his workmanship, created in Christ Jesus unto good works, which God hath before ordained that we should walk in them" (Ephesians 2:8-10).

Should I?

Some will object that if you live by Bible standards, you "lose your freedom." Nothing is further from the truth. Bible standards build walls so that things that would enslave us and destroy us cannot reach us. Sin is what binds. Romans 6:16 teaches *"Know ye not, that to whom ye yield yourselves servants to obey, his servants ye are to whom ye obey; whether of sin unto death, or of obedience unto righteousness?"* A man may say, "No one will tell me what to do! I am free to do drugs or drink alcohol or gamble or ___ if I want to." And he can commit those sins, but when he does, he becomes enslaved by those sins. The Christian living in God's plan is the one who has freedom.

Some today are teaching that separation and holy living are no longer important. They say we should only be concerned about doctrine and only separate over doctrine. They say that as long as we are saved, we are brothers in Christ. Certainly, we are brothers with all Christians. However, the word *doctrine* means "teaching," and the same Bible that teaches salvation by grace through faith (plus nothing), also teaches holy living, standards, and separation. These are teachings or doctrines of the Bible also. And while you can still go to Heaven if you are wrong on drinking alcohol, dressing immodestly or gambling, that does not mean that God does not think they are important. In fact, He thought they were important enough to condemn them in His Word.

God has saved us to glorify Him. We should seek to separate from anything, any practice, or anyone who would hinder us in fulfilling that purpose for our lives. The purpose of separation is so that we can accomplish what God wants us to accomplish.

WORKS CITED

Allison, Mike. *Preaching Standards: Right or Wrong?* Murfreesboro, Tennessee: Sword of the Lord Publishers, 2012.

Hyles, Jack. *Jack Hyles Speaks on Biblical Separation.* Hammond, Indiana: Hyles-Anderson Publishers, 1984.

Ironside, H. A. *Notes on the Book of Proverbs.* Neptune, N.J.: Loizeaux Brothers, 1908.

Pfeiffer, Charles F. & Everett F. Harrison. *The Wycliffe Bible Commentary.* Chicago: Moody Press, 1962.

Rice, John R. *The Double Curse of Booze.* Murfreesboro, Tennessee: Sword of the Lord Publishers, 1960.

Wallace, Tom. *The Christian and Social Issues.* Self-published, n.d.